AF880666

THE LAST BATTLESHIP

The Story of the USS *Missouri* (BB-63)

By Commander Scott C. S. Stone (USNR Ret.)

THE
DONNING COMPANY
PUBLISHERS

Cover: The big guns in action in 1991
during the war in the Persian Gulf.
U.S. Navy photo.

This book is dedicated, with enormous respect, to all those men who went to sea in the great battleship USS Missouri, *and who when called upon willingly put themselves in hazard for their country.*

Copyright © 1999 by Scott C. S. Stone
Second printing 2001
Third printing 2004
Fourth printing 2012

All rights reserved, including the right to reproduce this work in any form whatsoever without permission in writing from the publisher, except for brief passages in connection with a review. For information, write:

The Donning Company/Publisher
184 Business Park Drive, Suite 206
Virginia Beach, VA 23462

Steve Mull, General Manager
Barbara B. Buchanan, Office Manager
Barbara A. Bolton, Project Director
Pam Forrester, Project Research Coordinator
Sally C. Davis, Editor
Lori Wiley, Graphic Designer
Chad Casey, Reprint Graphic Designer
John Harrell, Imaging Artist
Priscilla Odango, Reprint Imaging Artist
Mary Ellen Wheeler, Proofreader/Editorial Assistant
Scott Rule, Director of Marketing
Travis Gallup, Marketing Coordinator

Library of Congress Cataloging-in-Publication Data:

Stone, Scott C. S., 1932–
The last battleship : the story of the USS Missouri (BB-63) / by Scott C. S. Stone.
p. cm.
ISBN 1-57864-082-2 (softcover : alk. paper)
1. Missouri (Battleship : BB 63)—History. I. Title.
VA 65.M59S76 1999
359.3'252'0973—dc21 99-34992
CIP

Printed in the United States of America
by Walsworth Publishing Company

S**eptember 2, 1945:** *the last battleship commissioned by the U.S. Navy lay lean and menacing in Tokyo Bay, surrounded by other vessels and anchored close to the spot where America's Commodore Matthew Perry had positioned his fleet in 1853. Perry's mission had been to open Japan to the West. Now, on the 01 veranda deck of the battleship USS* Missouri *(BB-63) stood eleven Japanese dignitaries, come to surrender to Allied powers at the close of World War II.*

Fleet Admiral Chester W. Nimitz was there to accept the surrender for America, along with General of the Army Douglas MacArthur and several Allied leaders. The day was overcast, with rain threatening. At 9:02 a.m. MacArthur spoke into a microphone ". . . we are gathered here . . . to conclude a solemn agreement whereby peace may be restored. . . ." The dignitaries signed the instrument of surrender, and the sun suddenly broke through the clouds.

Later, the vessels steamed out of Tokyo Bay, many of them to decommissioning and the end of active service. For the USS Missouri *the surrender ceremony on her deck was a memorable moment but not the end of her usefulness. Miles and miles of water would pass under her hull before her last assignment—to lie in sun-lit splendor in the shelter of Pearl Harbor, Hawaii, not far from another battleship, the USS* Arizona *(BB-39). These great dreadnoughts illuminate for all time a striking symmetry, representing, for America, the beginning and the end of the greatest conflict in human history.*

During keel laying ceremonies at the New York Navy Yard, 6 January 1941, Rear Admiral Clark Woodward, Commandant of the Navy Yard (second from right), drives in the first rivet. U.S. Navy photo.

BEGINNINGS

It was a totally unexpected honor, but Margaret Truman was thrilled to be selected to help launch the battleship named for her state. Equally surprised was her father, Senator Harry S. Truman. Margaret, then nineteen years old and a college sophomore, made the trip from Washington, D.C., to the New York Naval Shipyard where at least twenty thousand people had gathered to watch the ceremonies. On January 29, 1944, Margaret Truman dutifully smashed a bottle of champagne—made from Missouri grapes—against the gray steel of the newest battleship and watched as it slid down the incline and into the East River.

Long before the ceremony— as far back as January 1941—the keel was laid for the newest dreadnought, one of four to become famous as the Iowa class of battleships and including the USS *Iowa* (BB-61), USS *New Jersey* (BB-62), USS *Wisconsin* (BB-64), and the latest (and last), the USS *Missouri* (BB-63). Although the *Wisconsin*

started construction later and had a higher hull number, the *Missouri* was the last battleship built to completion.

At the ceremony Senator Truman remarked that "the time is surely coming when the *Missouri* and her sister ships, with batteries blazing, sail into Tokyo Bay." Meanwhile, millions of man-hours were going into readying the ship for war-time service, and crews were being trained in gunnery, navigation, seamanship, firefighting, and all the myriad skills required to sail and fight a ship nearly nine hundred feet long. On June 11, 1944, a second ceremony was held at the New York Navy Yard to officially commission the ship. Sailors raised the commissioning pennant and the battleship at once achieved the status of a fighting ship of the U.S. Navy. It was just five days after the Allied landing in Normandy, and there were no doubts the *Missouri* would see action.

The ship underwent the customary dock trials in Brooklyn, went into drydock in Bayonne, New Jersey, for a brief time, went on to Gravesend Bay in New York Harbor to take on ammunition, then steamed out into the Atlantic. Under the command of her first skipper, Captain William M. Callaghan, the *Missouri*, all ceremonies now behind her, began the tasks of firing her guns, testing her navigational equipment, and training

Left: Miss Margaret Truman, *Missouri's* sponsor, prepares to christen the ship at the New York Navy Yard, 29 January 1944. Looking on are (left to right): Rear Admiral Monroe R. Kelly, New York Navy Yard Commandant; Rear Admiral Sherman S. Kennedy, USN; and Senator Harry S. Truman of Missouri, the sponsor's father. Photo from National Archives.

Below: The USS *Missouri* is launched, 29 January 1944, at the New York Navy Yard. U.S. Navy photo.

Soon after commissioning, the *Missouri* at sea with her distinctive camouflage paint. Photo from National Archives.

her crews. The shakedown cruise took the ship south in the waters off Venezuela and Trinidad. Then it was back to Bayonne for a brief stop before sailing to war.

She sailed on November 10, 1944, headed for the far Pacific. She squeezed her way through the locks of the Panama Canal and sailed on to Hunters Point at San Francisco, where she was divested of the old Atlantic Fleet paint job and given the coloration preferred by the Pacific Fleet—decks painted blue-gray to blend with the sea when seen from overhead, the hull a dark blue, and area above a haze gray. The ship also took on spotter aircraft—single-seat SC-l Curtiss Seahawks.

Days later the *Missouri* moved slowly into Pearl Harbor, all hands at attention as she sailed by the shattered hulk of the USS *Arizona*, a dark and twisted reminder of the war's violent beginnings. It was the first time the two great battleships would be in close proximity, but it would not be the last. Now, in late December of 1944, the *Arizona* already was becoming a national symbol, while the *Missouri* was just weeks away from carrying the war to the enemy's homeland. In early January 1945, the ship traveled in company with other warships to Ulithi in the Caroline Islands, and in mid-February, the *Missouri* sailed to take part in the war.

ACTION EAST

Task Force 58 stood off the coast of Japan, an armada that included a screen of cruisers and destroyers, the battleships *Missouri* and *Wisconsin*, and the aircraft carriers USS *Lexington*, USS *Hancock*, and USS *San Jacinto*. The great battleships were there to provide any fire support that might be necessary, but also to refuel the destroyers. From the deck of the *Missouri* the crew kept watch for any enemy aircraft attempting to approach the carriers, and from those carriers the aircraft poured aloft to stream over Tokyo, bringing fire and devastation.

The pounding of Honshu, the main island of Japan, continued until Task Force 58 was ordered to the Bonin Islands to support the invasion of a tiny place called Iwo Jima. Dutifully, the *Missouri* steamed with the other warships and on the evening of February 19 found herself more than thirty miles off the coast of Iwo Jima and suddenly under attack by a Japanese bomber. The bomber came directly for the ship, but at nearly ten thousand yards the ship's guns opened up and blew the bomber out of the air.

The incredible new invention, radar, enabled the ship to fire at targets that couldn't be seen, and allowed the *Missouri* to take under fire planes flying above the cloud cover. As a first combat patrol, it was an unqualified success, and the battleship was sent back to Ulithi for a break in the action before returning again to the war.

The battleship was once again in the role of defense against enemy aircraft. In mid-March the aircraft carrier *Enterprise*, steaming nearby, came under air attack, and suddenly a Japanese plane came within range of the battleship's guns and the *Missouri* opened fire, knocking the plane into the water. Meanwhile, the carriers continued to launch their aircraft against targets on Kyushu, one of the main islands of the Japanese homeland.

Another island was about to receive the full fury of the battleship's guns. Okinawa was the southernmost of the Japanese home islands, and a strategic site, the last island on the road to the invasion of Japan. The carriers and their protectors were diverted south to bombard Okinawa prior to a landing, and the *Missouri's* great firepower was to be put to use in a shore bombardment on the southern coast of the island. On March 24, the battleship unlimbered her guns, sent an SC-l Seahawk airborne as a spotter plane, and began to shoot. She was almost twelve miles offshore when the guns opened up, closing to less than ten miles. In company with her sister-ships *New Jersey* and *Wisconsin*, the *Missouri* unleashed a torrent of fire, shooting over the hills of the coastline, blowing up buildings and an ammunition depot.

On April 11, the Japanese brought the war to the *Missouri*. In mid-after-

In heavy seas, her twin five-inchers and quad-forties blazing, Battle of Okinawa.

noon a kamikaze pilot in a "Zeke" fighter targeted the ship and came in just below the main deck. The impact started a fire that was quickly extinguished but not before it sent up a dark tower of smoke. No one aboard the ship was killed. The next day the ship's chaplain held funeral services for the dead Japanese pilot.

Five days later the battleship was again under attack, as a swarm of Japanese planes harassed the *Missouri* for hours. Once again a persistent "Zeke" set sights on the ship and despite being hit, kept boring in while the ship's gunners poured fire into it. The aircraft got close enough to clip machinery on the ship's fantail, but then it crashed and blew apart. Two men on the ship were injured by flying metal.

Back again for a rest period, the ship received new orders, and steamed for Guam. There, on May 18, Admiral William F. (Bull) Halsey, Jr., came on board to make the *Missouri* his flagship as commander, Third Fleet. And it was Halsey's request for the battleships to do more than provide anti-aircraft support that got the *Missouri, Iowa,* and *Wisconsin,* in company with some cruisers and destroyers, a job that suited them all: bombardment.

THE MISSOURI IN STATISTICS

Length overall:	**887 feet, 3 inches**
Length at waterline:	**860 feet**
Beam:	**108 feet, 2 inches**
Draft (at full load):	**37 feet, 8.75 inches, while weighing 57,500 tons**
Maximum speed:	**33 knots (almost 38 miles per hour)**
Propulsion:	**Eight Babcock and Wilson boilers/four General Electric turbines**
Displacement:	**57,500 tons (in 1988)**
Crew:	**About 2,000**
First Commanding Officer:	**Captain William M. Callaghan, June 11, 1944–May 14, 1945**
Last Commanding Officer:	**Captain Albert Lee Kaiss, June 13, 1990–March 31, 1992 (Captain Kaiss also commanded the ship May 10–June 20, 1986**

Anchored in port during her shakedown cruise, August 1944.
A K-type blimp hangs overhead. Photo from National Archives.

The tension aboard the ships was palpable as they sailed through waters that were perfect for mines, and despite the mine worries, the ships unlimbered their big guns. Firing from at least fifteen miles away, the ships shattered targets on the northernmost main Japanese island of Hokkaido.The *Missouri's* falling shells devastated an iron works, hammerhead cranes, and a factory that made steel. Two days later the ships were again off the main island of Honshu, blasting away at industrial targets at Hitachi.

Meanwhile, carrier aircraft and Army Air Force planes continued to pour their bombs onto Japanese targets. On August 6, from an altitude of 32,000 feet, a B-29 dropped a 10-foot-long, 9,000-pound bomb called "Little Boy" on the city of Hiroshima and flattened four square miles of the city. The bomb had the explosive power of 20,000 tons of TNT and resulted in the ultimate deaths of nearly 200,000 people. A similar bomb called "Big Boy" was dropped on Nagasaki three days later, killing at least 75,000 Japanese. The atomic bombs had the desired effect, for on August 10 the Japanese bowed to the inevitable and sued for peace.

But on August 9, the kamikaze attacks were as fierce as ever, and one enemy plane was bent on destroying the carrier *Wasp*, not far from the *Missouri.* Surrounded by friendly ships, the battleship's field of fire was severely restricted and she could only

During the Battle of Okinawa, the *Missouri* was struck amidships by a low-flying kamikaze.

Photographed during her shakedown period in August 1944. U.S. Navy photo.

bring to action her forty-millimeter guns. Bring them she did, and the action was close enough for observers to see the ship's tracer bullets smashing into the kamikaze. The plane crashed in the wake of the *Wasp*, a symbolic end to the massive kamikaze raids and a symbolic end to Japanese power. All in all, the ship had shot down eleven Japanese planes. The next day, August 10, the *Missouri* received word that the Japanese government had agreed to the unconditional surrender terms as spelled out in a meeting of Allied leaders in Potsdam, Germany. President Harry S. Truman made an official announcement to that effect, and all that remained was to effect the Japanese surrender—and then occupy, and finally rehabilitate, Japan itself.

VICTORS AND VANQUISHED

The day of the Japanese surrender aboard the *Missouri* began as every sailor knew it would—by sprucing up the ship for the ceremonies. In the center of a formation of friendly ships, the *Missouri* was an awesome reminder of Allied sea-power, and now a gleaming one, with freshly scrubbed decks and a new coat of polish where necessary. A table was brought up from the mess deck and covered in green cloth; this was to be the table where the documents would be signed. Above the ship flew the five-star flags of both Fleet Admiral Nimitz and General MacArthur.

The eleven Japanese rode in an American destroyer out to the *Missouri*, then transferred to motor launches to be taken aboard the battleship. On the deck, they stood in three rows, while an array of Allied officers lined along a bulkhead, and ship's crewmen crowded the decks and gun turrets to watch the surrender. American brass included Nimitz, Halsey, and MacArthur, and General Joseph "Vinegar Joe" Stilwell, and Lieutenant General George Kenney, plus high-ranking officers from China, France, Russia, and Great Britain.

The Japanese civilians among their party were dressed in top hat and tails, the officers in uniform. Aboard the *Missouri* it had been decreed that the uniform of the day was to be casual, so the officers were in khakis, without ties, and the crew in undress whites. Timed practices of the surrender were held, and ceremonies set to

Above: During a training exercise the *Missouri* fires a salvo from the forward sixteen-inch/fifty-caliber gun turret. Photo from National Archives.

Left: She fires the center sixteen-inch/fifty-caliber Mark Seven gun of each of her forward turrets, during a night gunnery practice. Photo from National Archives.

begin at 9:00 A.M. Two hours before the scheduled beginning of the ceremony, a destroyer came alongside and transferred 170 newsmen and photographers to the Mighty Mo. A few minutes after 8:00 A.M., Admiral Nimitz arrived and was followed a half-hour later by General MacArthur. Despite all the rehearsals, the ceremony began at 9:02 A.M., two minutes late.

General MacArthur made a short, eloquent address, noting in part that "it is my earnest hope and indeed the hope of all mankind that from this solemn occasion a better world shall emerge out of the blood and carnage of the past. . . ." Then the Japanese signed the surrender documents, followed by the Allies, with MacArthur signing as supreme commander of the Allied Powers, and Nimitz signing as the representative of the United States. Finally, MacArthur turned to the Japanese delegation and said, "these proceedings are now closed." An overcast sky suddenly brightened with sunlight. Against that color, hundreds of American airplanes flew over the anchored ships, a heart-stopping symbolic act that demonstrated America's power, and a dramatic moment not lost on the Japanese. The war was over; it was time to rebuild.

During training gunnery exercises, the *Missouri* fires the center sixteen-inch/fifty-caliber guns of the forward turrets. Photo from National Archives.

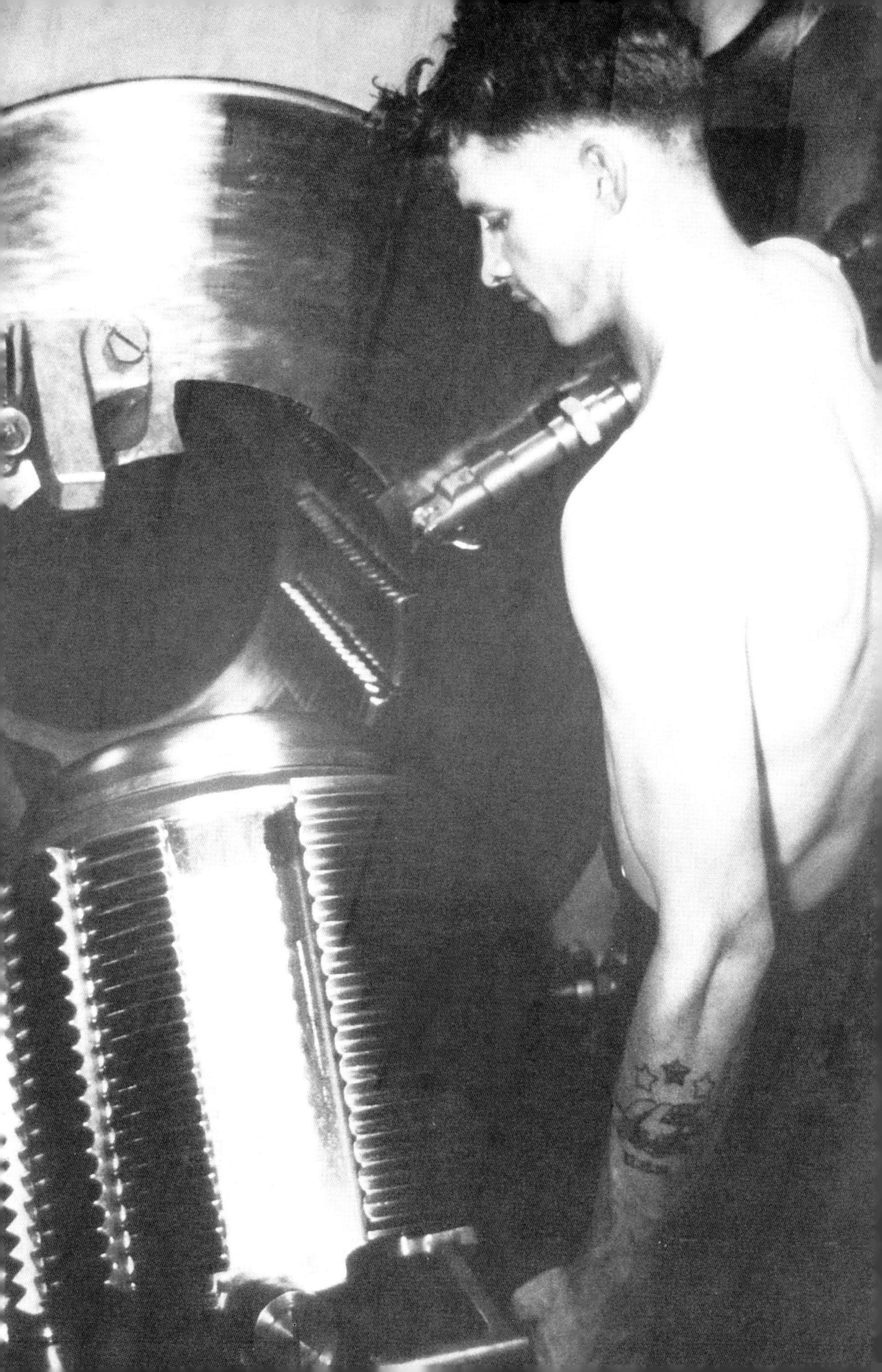

INTERLUDE

The great battleships had played their roles during the war, and it was now necessary to use them properly in peacetime. It was becoming increasingly clear that even their wartime uses would have to be carefully studied, for it was equally clear that sea power now was concentrated in the aircraft carriers that were potent air bases with no fixed address. How to mesh the great battleships with the carriers? And how would carrier admirals, all aviators, make practical use of ships built to bombard shorelines or fire on other enemy ships? Many of the great sea battles of World War II had taken place using carrier aircraft, sometimes without the opposing ships ever seeing each other. How would battleships fit into future sea battles?

The *Missouri*—some were calling it "The Mighty Mo"—sailed away from the historic surrender ceremony in Tokyo Bay and into warm Hawaiian waters. At Pearl Harbor, Admiral Nimitz came aboard again, this time to hold a reception. Then the Mighty Mo returned to her home port in Norfolk, where the bronze plaque was installed marking the surrender site. Shortly afterwards, the ship was moored at Pier 90, New York.

Now the ship's log grew filled with notations of a peacetime routine—moorings, taking on ammunition, and training exercises. An extensive cruise took the *Missouri* to the Mediterranean, and she called at ports in Turkey, Greece, Italy, Spanish Morocco, and Gibraltar. Throughout 1946 the ship seemed to be constantly in motion, in exercises, and in showing the flag in foreign ports.

The following year was more of the same, with a small added mission: in early September the ship took aboard President Truman and members of his family and carried them from Rio de Janeiro, Brazil, to Norfolk. There followed midshipman training cruises to England, Portugal, and France.

It was rather a pleasant time for the crews. Then disaster struck.

In a complicated series of events, the ship's officers were confused about the *Missouri's* position as the ship sailed off Hampton Roads, Virginia, on January 17, 1950. Hearings afterwards would show equipment failures and failures of judgment, all leading to one of the Navy's more embarrassing moments; shortly after 8:00 A.M., the powerful ship slid up onto a mud bank, her momentum carrying her some twenty-five hundred feet onto the shelf at Thimble Shoal. She was stuck fast.

Fire Controlman First Class E. M. Smith, gun captain of one of the ship's nine sixteen-inch/fifty-caliber Mark Seven main battery guns, opens his gun's breech plug. The gun's polished steel breech is stamped by its manufacturer, the Naval Gun Factory, Washington Navy Yard, D.C. Photo from National Archives.

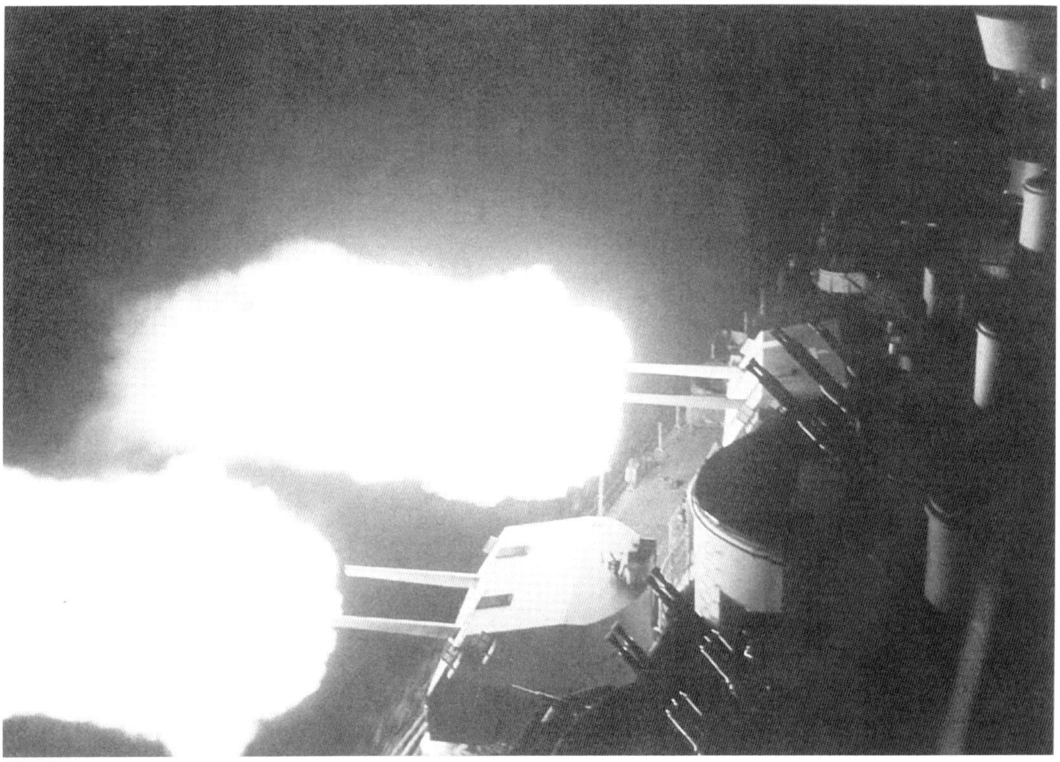

During a night gunnery practice, the ship fires her five-inch/thirty-eight-caliber secondary battery. Photo from National Archives.

There ensued heroic efforts to free the great battleship. Sixteen tugs, two fleet oilers (to take off the *Missouri's* fuel and lighten the ship), and an Army dredge began the recovery process, which was to lighten the ship, suck the mud from beneath her and make a channel to float the ship out again. Ammunition was off-loaded. Submarine rescue ships came alongside to provide power. Divers worked underwater with high-pressure hoses to soften the sand beneath the ship's hull. Pontoons were employed to raise the ship. It was an around-the-clock effort, and for a time it appeared that all the efforts were to be fruitless.

On February 1, the embarrassing ordeal came to an end. After fifteen days of enforced idleness on the mud bank, the powerful warship stirred slowly to life, pulled from the shore by the tugs at high tide, and the *Missouri* once again was afloat and at home in the sea.

The grounding received wide public attention, and was undoubtedly a black mark against the Navy. The actual physical damage to the Mighty Mo was far less than feared—she was repaired within a week at a cost of less than $50,000 and was speedily fit for sea. At the time probably no one thought her next major assignment would put her once more in the middle of a war.

SIGNIFICANT DATES IN THE MISSOURI HISTORY

1941—Keel laid at the New York Naval Shipyard, January 6.

1944—Launched by Margaret Truman, daughter of Senator (later President) Harry S. Truman, on January 29. Officially commissioned on June 11.

1944—Moored at Berth F-2, Ford Island, Pearl Harbor, Hawaii, December 24.

1945—Under way as part of Task Group 58.2, which included her sister battleship *Wisconsin*, aircraft carriers *Lexington, Hancock*, and *San Jacinto*, along with the cruisers *Boston* and *San Francisco*, and a destroyer screen, February 10. The task group conducted air strikes against Tokyo, supported the invasion of Iwo Jima and conducted air strikes on Okinawa.

1945—Under way with other Naval units conducting air strikes on Kyushu, joined in the shore bombardment of Okinawa, supported the invasion of Okinawa, March 16–May 5.

1945—Under way with other Naval units to join in the bombardment of Hokkaido on July 15, and a bombardment of Honshu July 17–18.

1945—Provided the site for the surrender of Japan to the Allies, ending World War II.

1945—Under way on various training exercises and fleet maneuvers, visiting Cuba, Gibraltar, Turkey, Greece, Italy, and Algeria before returning to the U.S. in May.

1950—Ran aground near Old Point Comfort, near Thimble Shoal Channel, at Hampton Roads, Virginia, January 17, going some twenty-five hundred feet onto a mud flat. The ship was refloated on February 1. In Inchon, Korea, firing bombardment missions, September 19. Visited by General of the Army Douglas MacArthur on September 21. Conducted shore bombardments on Korea, including Wonsan and Chongjin in company with other Navy units, October–December.

1951—Operations in Korean waters, including significant bombardment of enemy positions in Korea, January–March.

1952—Cruises to Cuba, Haiti, Norway, and England, January–April. Second assignment in Korean waters, October–December, in which the ship bombarded Wonsan and Tanchon.

1953—Operating off the east coast of Korea, again bombarding Wonsan as well as Suwon Dam, January–March.

1953—Training cruises to Brazil, Panama, and Cuba, June–August.

1954—Midshipman cruises by all four *Iowa*-class battleships to Portugal, France, and Cuba, June–August.

1955—The *Missouri* decommissioned and placed in mothballs at the Puget Sound Naval Shipyard, February 26.

1984—Towed to drydock and moored at the Long Beach Naval Shipyard, May–December.

1986—The ship is reactivated and given sea trials. The *Missouri* was commissioned again on May 10 by then-Secretary of Defense Caspar Weinberger. Later in the year, the battleship made cruises to Australia, Egypt, Turkey, Italy, and Spain, again transited the Panama Canal and moored again at the Long Beach Naval Station on December 19. It was an around-the-world shakedown cruise and the first battleship to circumnavigate the world since President Theodore Roosevelt's "Great White Fleet" of 1907.

1987—Operating in the North Arabian Sea and the Gulf of Oman, the ship and other Naval units supported the Allied convoy escort of tankers, September–November.

1991—Operated in Middle East waters in support of Operation Desert Storm, January 3–March 21. During this assignment the ship fired twenty-eight cruise missiles and 759 sixteen-inch shells.

1992—The *Missouri* is decommissioned for the second time; it happened March 31, and the ship subsequently was towed to her mothball fleet berth in Bremerton, Washington.

1995—The ship was removed from the Navy's registry, clearing the way for the battleship to be donated by the Navy for preservation as a memorial museum. The following year the caretaker for the historic ship was selected—the USS *Missouri* Memorial Association in Hawaii.

1998—The ship is towed from Bremerton by the tug *Sea Victory*, stopping at Astoria, Oregon, for a brief visit, then arriving at Pearl Harbor on June 22, to serve as a battleship memorial and museum.

ACTION EAST. . . AGAIN

It was a year to remember, 1950. President Truman escaped an assassination attempt outside of Blair House in Washington, D.C. The Soviets announced they had developed an atomic bomb. Chinese Communist forces invaded Tibet. German-born physicist Klaus Fuchs was found guilty of giving atomic secrets to the Russians, while President Truman advised the Atomic Energy Commission to go ahead with developing a hydrogen bomb. French forces withdrew from northern IndoChina and Senator Joseph McCarthy claimed to have a list of known Communists employed by the State Department. But for many, the pivotal point of that busy year was June 25, when North Korean troops poured over the border into South Korea.

The Korean War lasted three years and involved sixteen nations opposing Communist North Korea and Communist China. It was marked by a daring landing at Inchon on Korea's western coast, a move which caught Communist strategists completely off guard. But caught off guard in turn were the United Nations forces, which pushed into North Korea and up to the Yalu River, for there, having crossed the river, the troops encountered an onslaught of three hundred thousand Chinese and North Korean forces. The United Nations troops fled south to regroup, and going south as well were thousands of Korean refugees.

As the battleship enters port, a leadsman takes soundings. Photo from National Archives.

The *Missouri*, meanwhile, was in the process of recovering from the sarcasm and taunts that followed her grounding—some were calling her the "Muddy Mo"—and equally important, had survived some not-so-subtle attempts to get rid of her as being an anachronism and out of place in a modern Navy. The *Missouri* was about to prove her worth once again.

Weathering a savage hurricane in the Atlantic, the ship ran into a Pacific storm and then dodged a second one off Japan. Finally arriving in Korean waters, the ship sailed into a desperate situation—United Nations forces

The view off the battleship's portside during a high-speed run. Photo from National Archives.

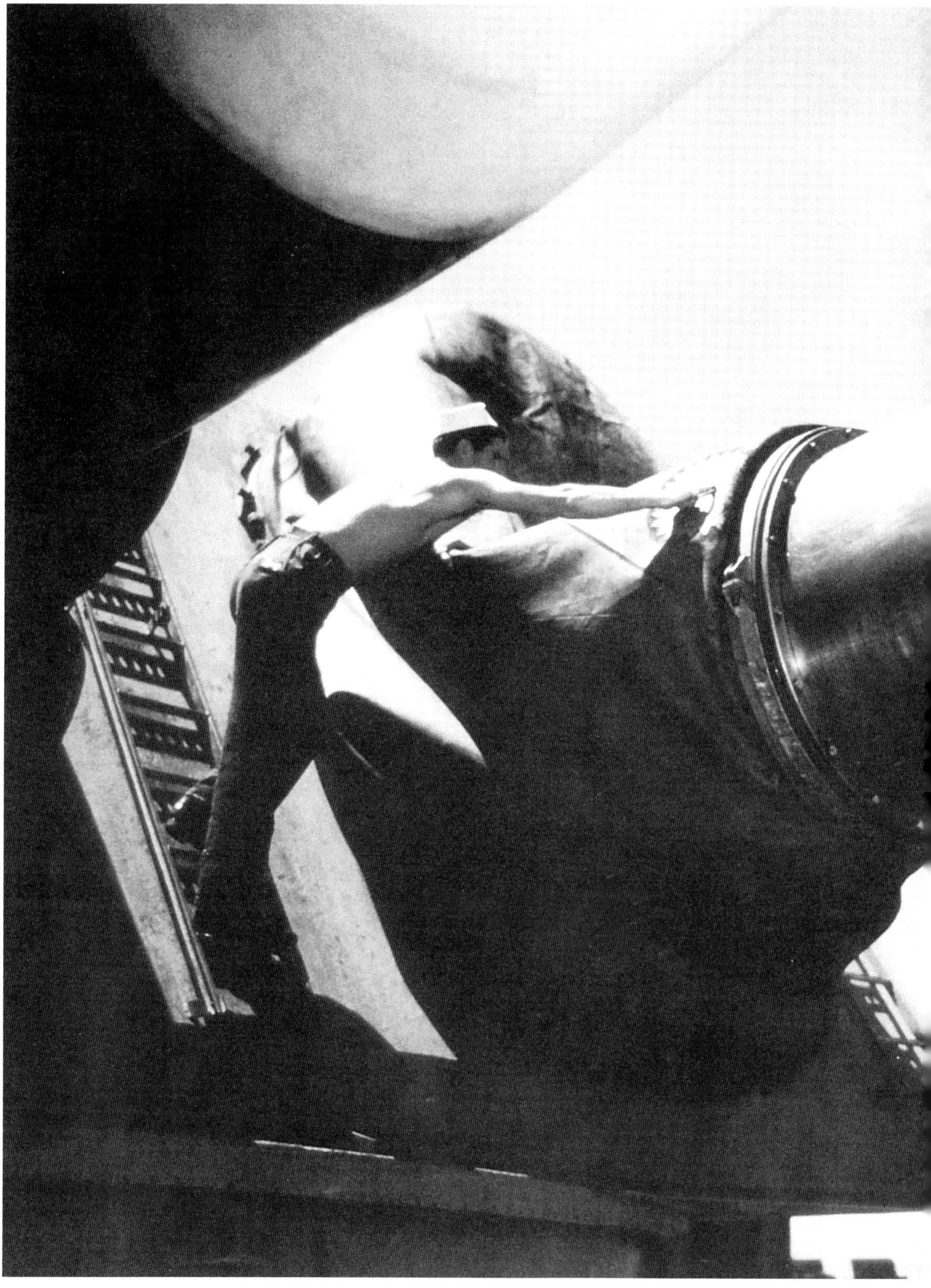

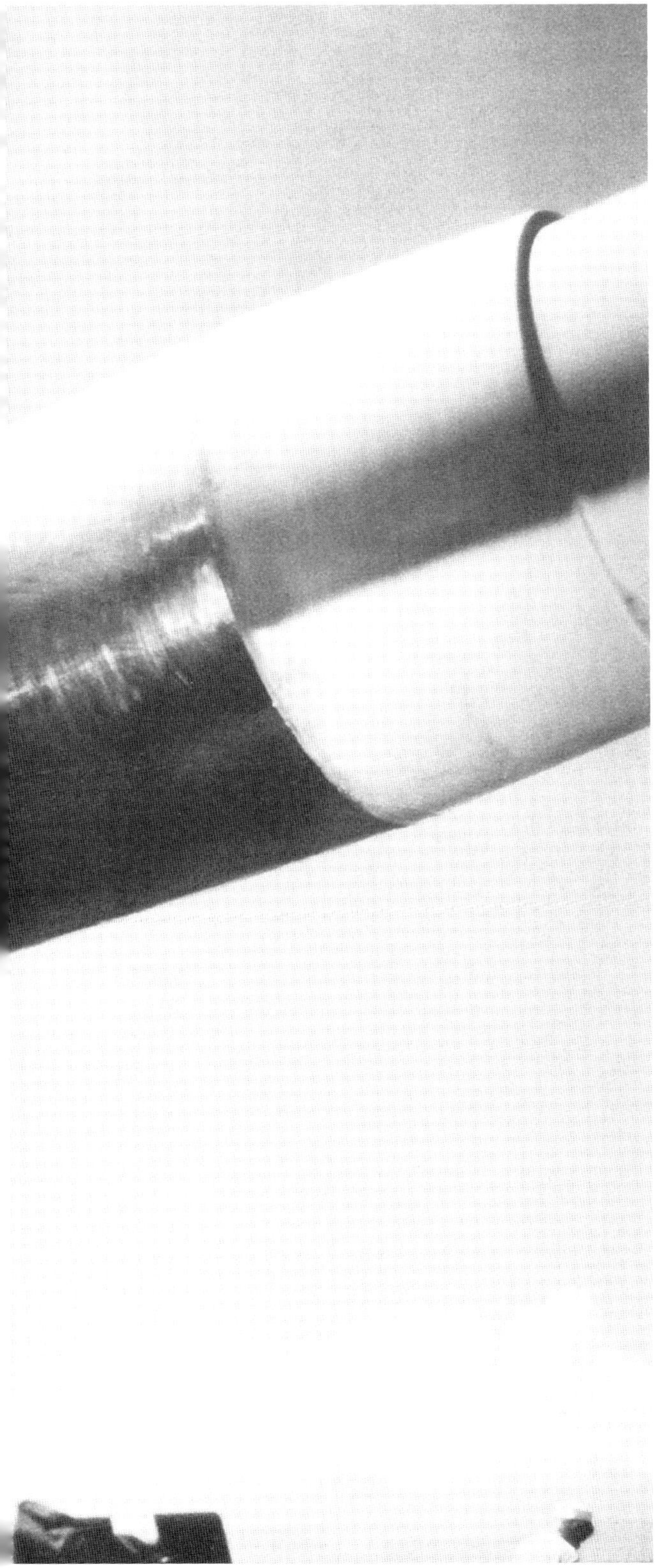

were hanging on grimly to a relatively small piece of land at the very tip of the Korean peninsula.

Off Korea's east coast, the *Missouri* trained her big guns on Samchok, smashing railroad bridges. The next day she blasted targets at Pohang. These were mere warming-up exercises for what was to follow, for the ship's real mission was to support MacArthur's bold amphibious landing at Inchon. That invasion went off as planned on September 15, and was an unqualified success, catching the North Korean forces completely by surprise. Soon they were on the roads and highways of Korea, streaming away to the north. The *Missouri* anchored south of the island of Wolmi-do in the Inchon Channel and began blazing away at enemy troops along the roads leading away from the Seoul-Inchon area.

The great battleship made her presence felt: she rained destruction on the North Korean seaport of Chongjin and the next day blasted Tanchon, another port. She served as flagship for the U.S. Seventh Fleet for part of this first Korean deployment, and was a welcome sight as she supported a landing at Wonsan. At Hungnam, where U.S. Marines converged after being surprised and heav-

While standing on the gun turret's face plate ladder, Fire Controlman Third Class James Tucker adjusts the canvas "bloomer" on a sixteen-inch/fifty-caliber gun. Photo from National Archives.

ily outnumbered at the Chosin Reservoir, the *Missouri* laid down a devastating nightime barrage that helped the evacuation of friendly troops. Then she was firing often and effectively at targets along the bleak east coast of Korea. Now and then the ship was able to pull back to rest in the harbor at Sasebo, Japan, which became her temporary home port, and finally, in late March 1951, the ship completed her deployment and headed back for Norfolk. She had fired nearly three thousand rounds from her sixteen-inch guns, and more than eight thousand rounds from her five-inch guns, and was a potent force for the United Nations in the early part of the war.

Back in the United States, the ship segued smoothly into the role of training vessel for midshipman cruises, sailing to Oslo where the ship's officers, crews, and midshipmen alike were enthralled by Norwegian hospitality. On to Cherbourg in France, where the crew was able to get to Paris, and then the Mighty Mo returned to Norfolk. It was the calm before the storm, for in September 1952, the battleship was ordered back to the cold waters and the biting wind and the bleak hills of Korea. The war was far from over.

Back at the familiar port of Yokosuka, Japan, the *Missouri* once again became a flagship as Vice Admiral Joseph J. Clark, commander Seventh Fleet, and his staff came aboard the ship. Less than two weeks later the Mighty Mo lay off the rugged Korean coast and trained her guns on enemy shore installations, and the list of her victims grew—Tanchon, Wonsan, Chongjin, Hamhung, Songjin, and others. It was off Taedol-li that a spotter helicopter from the Mighty Mo went down in enemy territory, and three *Missouri* men, including the pilot and two Marine Corps officers, were lost.

Operating as part of Task Force 77, the ship continued to blast away at enemy shore positions into the new year. Early the following March, as the ship was maneuvering in deep Wonsan Harbor, enemy shore batteries opened up and peppered the ship with shrapnel. The *Missouri* took no direct hits because the enemy shells were bursting in the air. Five days later the ship was fired on by 105-millimeter guns, again in Wonsan Harbor, and the enemy probably regretted it for the Mighty Mo unleashed its five-inch guns and poured back nearly a thousand rounds. A few days later the ship fired on targets in the Wonsan area and headed back for Sasebo. Entering the harbor, the ship suffered an unexpected tragedy: on the bridge the skipper, Captain Warner Edsall, dropped dead of a heart attack, and the crew mourned.

Her deployment ended, the *Missouri* headed home.

A Vought OS2U Kingfisher floatplane is hoisted on board after a flight. Photo from National Archives.

It was a different homecoming from the euphoria of the ending of World War II. The Korean War—not even called a war but a "police action"—was in a far place at the wrong time and already was on its way to becoming "the forgotten war." It was not that the American public was opposed to the war; it was indifferent to it. On July 27, 1953, an armistice was signed at a little hamlet in central Korea called Panmunjom, which according to folklore was once a famous trysting place for lovers. Despite the world's indifference, the war had been devastating: United Nations casualties were 344,227, including 25,604 American dead and 103,492 wounded. North Korean and Chinese Communist dead and wounded totaled 1,540,000. At least 2,000,000 civilians were killed and thousands left homeless.

There was an armistice but no peace treaty. More than forty years after the fighting, there still was no peace treaty and tensions continued on the Korean peninsula. The *Missouri* sailed home having done her share to end the war that was strangely unremembered.

For the remainder of 1953 and throughout 1954 the Mighty Mo reverted to her old peacetime duties, taking midshipmen on training cruises, training new crewmen, and showing the flag. In June 1954, there was a glorious time to gladden the heart of an old battleship sailor—getting underway for Portugal as part of Task Group 40, the crew of the *Missouri* could look over the water during tactical training exercises and see all three of her sister ships, the USS *Iowa*, USS *New Jersey*, and the USS *Wisconsin*. It was the only time all four sailed together.

Back from Europe the Mighty Mo went into the Norfolk Naval Shipyard for a much-needed overhaul, then on to more exercises around Cuba and Haiti. Then the rumors began, as usual well ahead of the official word. The *Missouri* was to be decommissioned.

The journey seemed a long one to the ship's officers and crew, a trip that took them once more through the Panama Canal, on to Long Beach, San Francisco, and Seattle. At Bangor, Washington, the ship off-loaded ammunition and in mid-September was anchored at Bremerton. A few days later the ship was drydocked at the Puget Sound Naval Shipyard. All along what was thought to be the final journey, thousands of people turned out to visit the historic ship. In San Francisco alone more than twenty thousand jammed the ship but one visitor got particular attention. He was Fleet Admiral Nimitz, whose most notable visit had been nine years earlier when he accepted, for America, the surrender of the Japanese aboard the ship in Tokyo Bay.

Weeks of hard work followed the ship's arrival in the Northwest—it was

Work party loading onions during a training cruise. Photo from National Archives.

surprisingly hard and complicated to put the *Missouri* in mothballs. Before the vessel could be buttoned up, repairs had to be made, off-loading of some equipment had to take place, and the inevitable inventorying. All gear was cleaned and preservatives applied for the ship's long sleep.

On February 26, 1955, the ship's flags were hauled down. Down fluttered the stars and stripes from the flagstaff at the ship's stern, and down from the mast came the commissioning pennant. At that moment the *Missouri* was no longer a part of the active navy. But her mothballing had been done over a period of nearly six months and had been accomplished with care, for who knew if or when this great battleship would be called on to serve again?

THE FIREPOWER

The Missouri was built with nine sixteen-inch/fifty-caliber guns in three triple turrets.

She also carried twenty five-inch/thirty-eight-caliber guns in ten twin mounts, but this was reduced in the 1984–1986 modernization period to twelve guns in six twin mounts.

Also on board were eighty forty-millimeter guns in twenty quad mounts. All the quad mounts were taken off the ship in the 1984–1986 modernization.

On board were forty-nine twenty-millimeter guns in single mounts, reduced to twenty-two by 1947. Dual-mount twenty-millimeter guns were brought on board, starting with eight in 1945 and ending with thirty-two during the Korean War. All were eliminated before the first decommissioning in 1955.

During the 1984–1986 modernization, four Vulcan/Phalanx Gatling guns were added, as were four Harpoon antiship missile canisters with a total of sixteen missiles, plus eight quadruple Tomahawk launchers, for a total of thirty-two missiles.

Above: Seated before a forty-millimeter gun tub lined with stowed helmets, a crew member reads the Public Affairs Committee's Publication, "What About Girls?" Photo from National Archives.

Right: Dental officers, Commander Jessie B. Bancroft and Lieutenant George E. Wheeler, at work in the battleship's dental spaces. Photo from National Archives.

WAKING THE GIANT

At Bremerton the ship was a tourist attraction, visited by thousands. Local civic leaders became aware of the ship's drawing power. Hollywood discovered the vessel as well, and a couple of movies were filmed in part on her deck. In time the ship's wardroom was opened to display for visitors scenes from the *Missouri's* past via an extensive photo display. In other ways the ship was rigged so visitors who were barred from sensitive areas of the ship could at least peek through doors or through plastic sheeting.

From early 1955 to early 1984 the ship waited. Finally the word came down: the historic vessel was to be reactivated and put back into service and former *Missouri* crewmen, wherever they were, surely smiled at the news. On May 14, tugboats pulled the somnolent ship away from the pier and into the waters of Puget Sound and got her on her way to the Long Beach (California) Naval Shipyard. After eleven days at sea the ship arrived and the work of getting her ready for sea began in earnest. Already the *Iowa* and *New Jersey* had been put back into service and the *Wisconsin* would follow, part of a Navy plan for rebuilding the fleet, which had fallen off in the years after the fighting in Korea.

To keep the ship modern and as offensively potent as possible, some

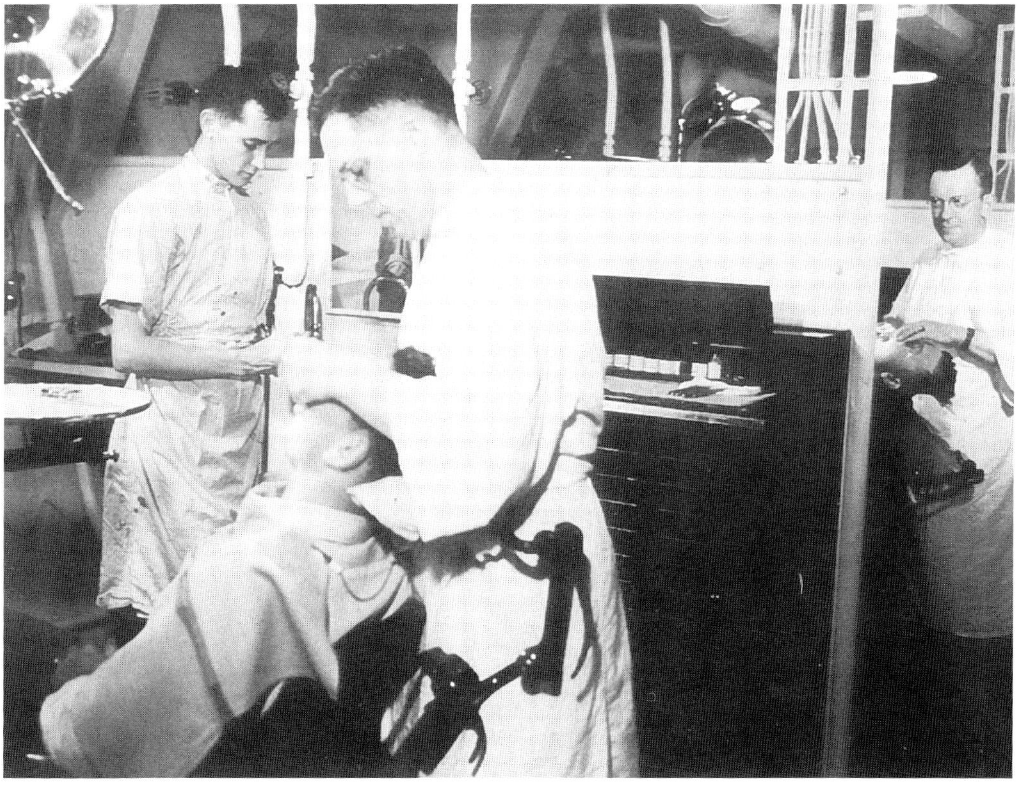

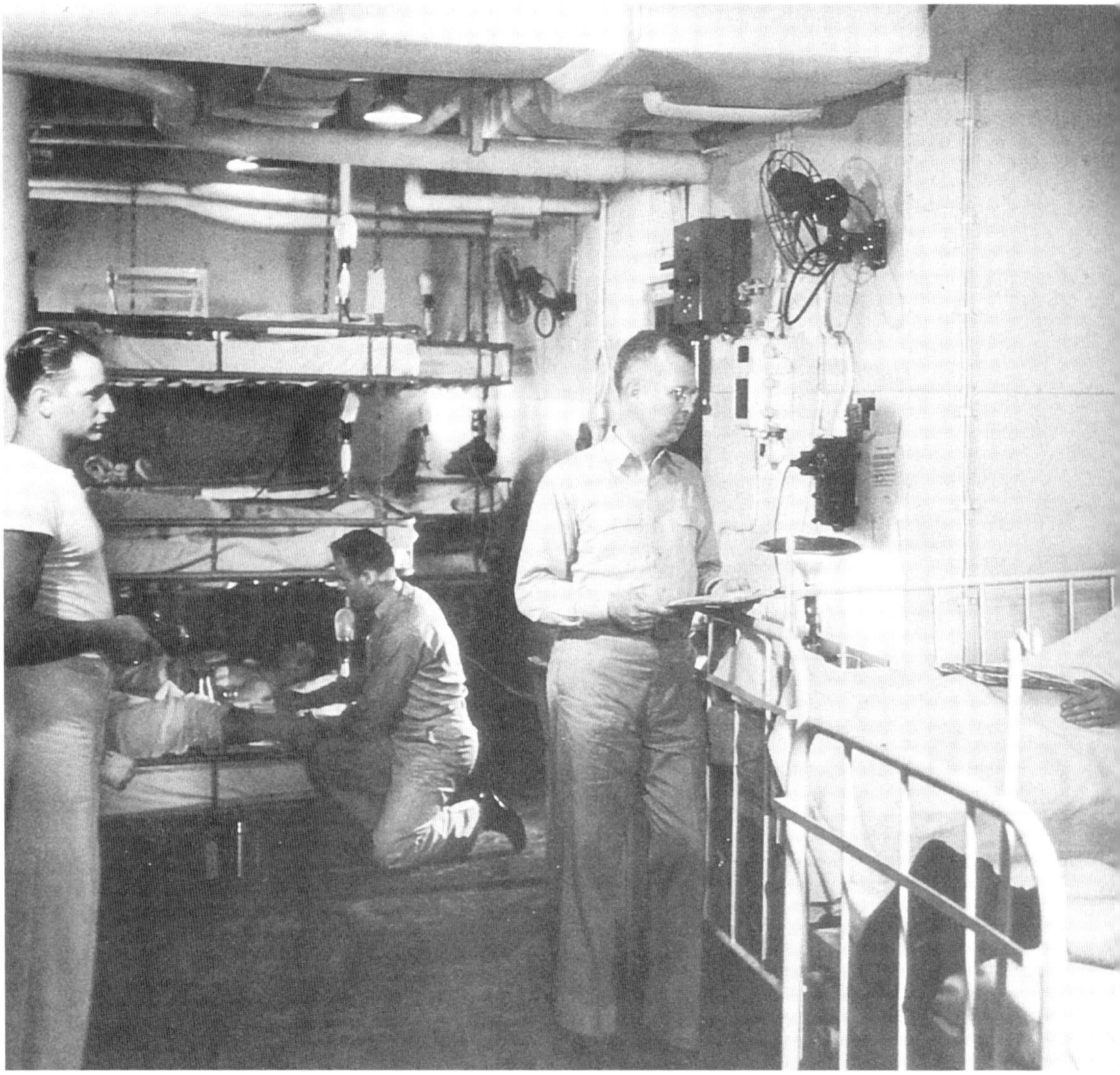

Commander Louis E. Gilge, Medical Corps, makes his rounds in the battleship's sick bay as Pharmacist's Mate Second Class Frank Mancini stands by at left. Photo from National Archives.

vintage guns were removed and some modern missile systems added. All the quad forty-millimeter mounts were taken off, and the twenty five-inch guns were reduced to twelve guns in six twin mounts. What came aboard were four Vulcan/Phalanx Gatling guns, four Harpoon anti-ship missile canisters with sixteen missiles, and eight quadruple Tomahawk cruise missile launchers.

On January 28, 1986, the ship got underway under her own power; then came the necessary sea trials in which all facets of the ship were tested, from guns to navigation equipment and engines to communications. The *Missouri* had come awake.

At pier 32 near the Oakland Bay Bridge, on a clear day in May 10, 1986, Secretary of Defense Caspar Weinberger placed the Mighty Mo back in commission as a crowd of more than ten thousand watched from the pier. For her shakedown cruise the ship drew an enviable assignment; she was to sail around the world on a goodwill tour and show the flag mission.

The Mighty Mo was sailing in the wake of another historic fleet, President Theodore Roosevelt's "Great White Fleet" of 1907, the *Missouri* being the first battleship to circumnavigate the world since that time. During the "Great White Fleet" cruise an earlier battleship named the *Missouri* went out of her way to salute the small Hawaiian island of Molokai as the result of a letter sent to President Theodore Roosevelt by one of the island's residents. Brother Joseph Dutton, Civil War veteran and highly patriotic, asked the president if the *Missouri* could divert from her course long enough to sail near Molokai's leper colony, where Brother Dutton worked on behalf of the lepers. Roosevelt agreed, and ordered it to happen. Now, in 1986, the modern *Missouri* sailed in the wake of her predecessor and dipped her flag in salute to the lepers of Molokai.

The cruise took the warship from Hawaii to Australia and on to Diego Garcia, that small island in the Indian Ocean, vital for its strategic location; then the ship traveled to Suez, transited the Suez Canal into the Mediterranean and went on to Turkey, Italy, Spain, Mallorca, and Portugal. Then it was Panama again, through the canal and finally, just in time for Christmas, the ship moored again at the Long Beach Naval Station—four months and thousands of miles later.

The new year, 1987, brought renewed activity. The Mighty Mo was at sea for gunfire qualification exercises, training exercises, exercises in conjunction with other vessels. August found her moored at Subic Bay in the Philippines, and there was little doubt she was to see action again. With cruisers, destroyers, and an oiler, the *Missouri* took part in exercises off Singapore and then transited the Straits of Malacca.

Operation Earnest Will was the Mighty Mo's next assignment, helping escort convoys of tankers in the Strait of Hormuz. The tankers were vulnerable to Iran's Silkworm missiles, and the *Missouri* was there as a deterrent. The ship would escort the tankers in the Gulf of Oman right up to the curving Strait of Hormuz, where smaller warships would accompany the tankers through the Straits and into

the Persian Gulf. For *Missouri* crewmen, it was long, hot duty, and after the tension of the first few trips, it became monotonous duty as well, until the ship was relieved by the carrier USS *Midway* and her battle group.

The months that followed slipped into years, but not idleness. The *Missouri* continued to train, to carry out battle problems at sea, and particularly to test her cruise missile capabilities. She operated off California, in Hawaiian waters, paid a visit to Vancouver, maneuvered with carriers and other ships, and in general accomplished what a Naval vessel in peacetime is supposed to do—prepare for war.

Machinist's Mate Second Class Reed Bankhead and Machinist's Mate First Class Ralph Weiss operating metal lathes in the battleship's machine shop. Photo from National Archives.

Right: As men rest and read in their bunks, other crew members get a drink of water from the quarter's scuttlebutt. Photo from National Archives.

December 1990, found the *Missouri* anchored off Pattaya Beach, in Thailand. Late December found her en route to the Persian Gulf, once again to fire her guns in anger.

ACTION . . . DESERT STORM

It was not what the crew expected; sailors had been looking forward to a cruise that was scheduled to take them to Korea, the Philippines, and Japan. And it was reported that following the cruise, the ship was to be decommissioned once again. Already the *Iowa* was ready for decommissioning and the *New Jersey's* inactivation was actually underway. For the *Missouri* it seemed just a matter of time, and not much time at that.

In the Middle East the Iraqi strongman Saddam Hussein made a bold but characteristic move. He sent three army divisions across the border into Kuwait on the pretense that Kuwait was really just another province of Iraq. The conquest was not difficult and soon the only question that remained was, would he invade Saudi Arabia as well?

In Washington, President George Bush began building a coalition of friendly Middle East powers to take military action if necessary.

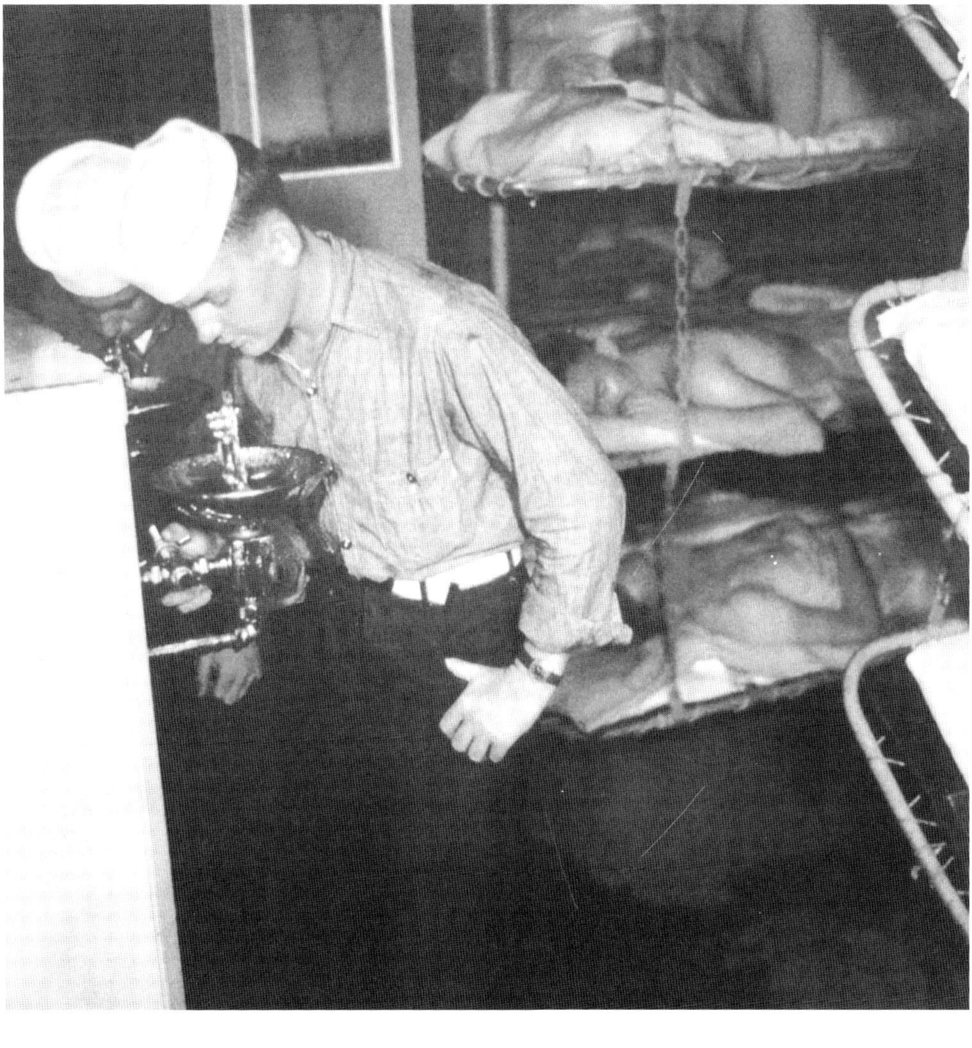

While operating off Okinawa on 11 April 1945, the ship is attacked by a Japanese A6M "Zero" kamikaze. The plane caused only minor damage and no casualties on the battleship. In the lower foreground a forty-millimeter quad gun mount's crew fires at attacking planes. Photo from National Archives.

THE SURRENDER PLAQUE

During a stopover in the Norfolk, Virginia, Navy Yard in October 1945, the Missouri received a permanent reminder of her place in history. Workmen in the yard installed a bronze plaque marking the site of the Japanese surrender on the 01 deck. The plaque reads:

U.S.S. MISSOURI. Over this spot on 2 September 1945 the instrument of formal surrender of Japan to the allied powers was signed thus bringing to a close the second world war. The ship at that time was at anchor in Tokyo Bay. Lattitude 35°21'17" North. Longitude 139°45' 36" East.

Everyone hoped it would not be necessary, and the U.S. sought political sanctions via the United Nations. When the coalition was in place and the U.N. had shown support, Saddam Hussein was given a deadline to pull out of Kuwait.

At midnight on January 15, 1991, the deadline expired and war was imminent. The next day Allied aircraft bombed Baghdad, leveling the palace, and also destroyed most of the air-defense system. The war had begun.

On January 3, the Mighty Mo had sailed into familiar territory, transiting the Strait of Hormuz and cruising into the Persian Gulf. In mid-month she was anchored at Manama, Bahrain, and on the sixteenth sailed into dangerous waters of the Gulf. One of the first acts of the ship's personnel was to destroy an Iraqi mine floating menacingly in waters where the ship was to operate.

In the early morning of January 17, in a dark night, the men of the *Missouri* went to general quarters and soon afterwards the first Tomahawk missile flashed away and headed for Baghdad. And another. And another. A half-dozen missiles were fired that night, adding to the devastation that Saddam Hussein's actions had brought down on his own people. In the next three days the ship continued firing her missiles, sending a total of twenty-eight Tomahawks toward targets in Iraq. There was a lull, then on February 3, at a place called Khafji, the ship fired her big guns.

Khafji was a deserted Saudi town, but the only junction on the coastal road leading to Kuwait City; Saddam's plan was to attack the city and draw U.S. forces north to rescue the trapped Saudi troops, then ambush the U.S. forces. Instead, Saddam's troops ran into U.S. Marines already on the site.

Steaming to her anchorage in Tokyo Bay for the formal signing of the Japanese surrender. A destroyer runs alongside, and beyond is the USS *Iowa*. This photograph was flown to Washington, D.C., directly from Japan, arriving on 2 September 1945, the day the Japanese surrender was signed. Photo from Naval Historical Center.

Surrender of Japan, Tokyo Bay, 2 September 1945. Standing in front: Foreign Minister Mamoru Shigemitsu (wearing top hat), and General Yoshijiro Umezu, chief of the Army General Staff. Behind them, in middle row, (left to right): Major General Yatsuji Nagai, Army; Katsuo Okazaki, Foreign Ministry; Rear Admiral Tadatoshi Tomioka, Navy; Toshikazu Kase, Foreign Ministry; and Lieutenant General Suichi Miyakazi, Army. In the back row (left to right): Rear Admiral Ichiro Yokoyama, Navy; Saburo Ota, Foreign Ministry; Captain Katsuo Shiba, Navy; and Colonel Kaziyi Sugita, Army. U.S. Army photo.

Right: Surrender of Japan, Tokyo Bay, 2 September 1945. General Yoshijiro Umezu, chief of the Army General Staff, signs the Instrument of Surrender on behalf of Japanese Imperial General Headquarters. Across the table are Lieutenant General Richard K. Sutherland, and General of the Army Douglas MacArthur. Representatives of the Allied powers are behind General MacArthur. Photo from National Archives.

A savage battle ensued and the Iraqis got the worst of it. But to prevent the Iraqi troops from receiving reinforcements, the big guns were brought in.

The *Missouri* moved close inshore to fire at bunkers, sending out RPV unmanned aircraft as a surveillance system. The big sixteen-inch guns fired for the first time since the Korean War, the projectiles streaking in the night and the gunfire like thunder rolling over the water. The unmanned RPV found targets and relayed the data back so the guns could open up. The next night the battleship was back, hurling the heavy shells at on-shore targets. The shelling wiped out troop concentrations and silenced an artillery battery. In three days of shooting the *Missouri* hurled 112 rounds of sixteen-inch shells.

Relieved for a few days by her sister ship *Wisconsin,* the *Missouri* returned to Khafji within a few days and resumed her duties; she owned the biggest Naval guns afloat and used them to rain destruction on a variety of enemy targets. At one point the Iraqis fired back, several rounds falling in the water alongside the ship but none scoring a hit.

A few days later the Mighty Mo was selected to feint at a point on the Kuwait coast. Captain Peter Bulkeley, as commander of the Task Group, came aboard the ship and directed her to an area where the ship fired on enemy troops on an island. The Iraqis

Fleet Admiral Chester W. Nimitz, USN, signs the Instrument of Surrender as United States representative. Directly behind him (left to right): General of the Army Douglas MacArthur; Admiral William F. Halsey, USN; and Rear Admiral Forrest Sherman, USN. Photo from National Archives.

Right: During the surrender ceremonies, Tokyo Bay, U.S. Navy carrier planes fly in formation over USS *Missouri* (BB-63). Aircraft types include F4U, TBM, and SB2C. Ship in the distance is USS *Ancon* (AGC-4). Photo from National Archives.

took the bait and moved troops and equipment to the area, where they expected an invasion. Then, a second time, the *Missouri* was used in a feint as Coalition troops began the ground war to retake Kuwait. The ship lay offshore and hurled round after round of sixteen-inch projectiles.

There was a harrowing moment. The ship's skipper looked up one dark night to see a Silkworm missile heading toward the *Missouri.* Glowing with an unearthly light, the missile hurtled toward the battleship. The ship's electronic tracking system decided the missile was not coming close enough to be a threat, although every man aboard knew differently. The crew hit the deck and waited.

Patrolling nearby was the British

At anchor in Tokyo Bay, the day that the Japanese surrender ceremonies were held on her deck. U.S. Army photo.

frigate HMS *Gloucester*, which tracked the missile and had no doubts the American battleship was in grave danger. Acting quickly, the frigate fired two anti-aircraft missiles, one of which hit the Silkworm missile and destroyed it in the air. The *Missouri's* unmanned RPV spotter plane located the missile battery and soon the ship's big guns silenced it forever.

Coalition units were rolling up the Iraqi forces at a remarkable rate, and the Mighty Mo stayed on the move to remain positioned to fire ahead of the advancing friendly troops. Firing at targets, often at night, the ship threw 759 rounds at enemy targets during the action, a colossal bombardment both deadly and intimidating. On February 28, the short-lived war came to an end, and the Mighty Mo eased back to Bahrain. Not long after, the ship left the Persian Gulf through the Strait of Hormuz and sailed majestically out into the Indian Ocean. She had been to her third war, performed as admirably as usual, and now she was going home. The war was over. Six months to the day she left, the *Missouri* arrived back in Long Beach, to a tumultuous welcome.

Along the way home the ship stopped in Australia and Hawaii, and it seemed that rumors followed in her wake. The *Wisconsin* was mothballed by the end of September, as a period of attrition began in the military, and it seemed that the *Missouri's* active service was about to end as well. There was credence to the rumors, for the American public was in a mood to cut military spending. Before long there was no doubt about it, the Mighty Mo was to be decommissioned for the second time.

Before that would happen, the *Missouri* made a sentimental journey. She sailed back to Hawaii to take part in observances of the fiftieth anniversary of the Japanese attack on the U.S. Pacific Fleet at Pearl Harbor. On December 7, 1991, President George Bush came aboard after ceremonies on the *Arizona* Memorial, and made a brief talk from the 01 deck where the Japanese surrender had taken place. It was a calm, sun-lit morning not unlike the one fifty years earlier, before the fury of the surprise attack. Dignitaries gathered, including some of the surviving crewmembers of the *Arizona*. Receptions were held, and sailors gathered to talk shop about ships, particularly the great battleships, soon to disappear from the seas.

A few days later the *Missouri* weighed anchor and set a course for California. She arrived at Seal Beach and off-loaded ammunition, then went on to her home port at Long Beach. She was to have, after long service, the well-deserved rest of a warrior.

Still, the ship was not left to decay. Measures were taken to guard against rust and corrosion. Unnecessary parts were removed, although some pieces, such as the Tomahawk launchers, were left in place. All through the early part of 1992 the great ship lay quiet as she

was prepared for deactivation, and on March 31, the crew turned out in dress blues and the ship was rigged with colorful bunting as the decommissioning ceremony began. There were speeches and a prayer. *Taps* was played and the flags lowered and the crew filed off the ship.

The last to leave was the skipper, Captain Albert Lee Kaiss, who had been commanding officer when the ship was recommissioned, and now commanded as the ship was being removed from the active list. He walked away, the last captain of the last battleship.

THE RIVALRIES

The battleship that now had been involved in three wars found herself at the center of yet another—the rivalry to secure the ship for all time. Cities were battling to have the *Missouri* for its historic value, as a memorial, and as a vessel that would be frequently visited.

In Hawaii, interest in the ship went back to 1984. In that year an organization was formed by community leaders, retired Navy personnel, and supporters of the Navy League; the purpose was to secure the *Missouri* and her battle group by promoting Pearl Harbor as the home port. At that time the ship was newly recommissioned and Pearl Harbor seemed a natural choice for her home port. One argument was the close relationship between the Navy and the Hawaii civilian community.

The second decommissioning of the Mighty Mo put an end to hopes of having the battle group home-ported at Pearl Harbor, but did not lessen

Left: The *Missouri* rounds the east end of Ford Island, Pearl Harbor, in late September 1945. Photo from National Archives.

Below: Anchored off Piraeus, Greece, April 1946. Photo from National Archives.

Hawaii's interest in the battleship. In preparation for the ship's presence, an infrastructure had been put into place to handle the ship and her crew, notably the completion of a pier at F-5 on Ford Island in the middle of Pearl Harbor.

When it was apparent the ship would not be commissioned again, interest shifted to securing the Mighty Mo as a memorial itself—it would make for "historic bookends" to have both the *Arizona* and the *Missouri* available in proximity. In 1994 the USS *Missouri* Memorial Association was chartered to seek the donation of the battleship for Pearl Harbor. In addition to the powerful argument of the nearby *Arizona*, there was the fact that the Mighty Mo in Pearl Harbor would be under Navy control in a historic environment. Additionally, adjacent to the *Arizona* was another historic vessel, the submarine USS *Bowfin*, an interesting memorial and museum.

Thus the Hawaii contingent's great argument was that the site could offer more than other places with the powerful added argument of history. Those other places, however, were eager to have the Mighty Mo, and

In port, circa 1948, a motor launch with U.S. Naval Academy Midshipmen passes in the foreground. Photo from Naval Historical Center.

Run aground on Thimble Shoals, Virginia, 17 January 1950, it was 1 February 1950 before she was freed. Here several harbor tugs work to refloat her while mine-sweepers and other ships pass to her stern in the shipping channel. Photo from National Archives.

Opposite page: Underway at sea during fleet maneuvers, March 1950. Photo from National Archives.

would not give up without a fight. The ship's old home port of Long Beach sought the vessel. So did San Francisco, a great maritime city in its own right, and so did Bremerton, where the ship already was physically located.

In January 1996, the *Missouri* was removed from the Navy registry, making it possible for the Navy to donate the ship as a memorial to one of the competing cities. The competition intensified. In Hawaii, about $8 million in loans and donations was raised to get the ship to the Islands and get it ready for visitors. Meanwhile, the Navy was expressing its concerns to all the competing cities—the cities would have to show how the ship would be moved from Bremerton without damage, protected while being towed, and finally how it would be operated without slipping into debt. In Hawaii in 1996, the USS *Missouri* Memorial Association was confident. The association chairman, Ed Carter, told a reporter that "we think our position for the *Missouri* is so compelling that the Navy only has one way to go on this."

Events bore him out. On August 21, 1996, Secretary of the Navy John H. Dalton announced that the Navy had selected the USS *Missouri* Memorial Association to acquire the ship and operate it as a memorial and museum. "This was a very tough decision," Dalton said, "since all the proposals were so excellent and impressive." From his Hawaii headquarters, Admiral R. J. Zlatoper, commander in chief, U.S. Pacific Fleet, said, "*Missouri* not only symbolizes the end of a tragic war, but also our commitment to

maintaining peace and stability in the region."

In the city of Bremerton, the Navy's choice of Pearl Harbor was not accepted without a fight. Congressmen from Washington battled to have the selection process reopened, but their effort was defeated in the Senate, 53–46. As he had from the beginning, Hawaii's senior senator, Daniel K. Inouye, spearheaded the congressional fight to get and keep the Mighty Mo in Hawaii. Said Inouye, "I am pleased that the Senate made the right decision this evening. The USS *Missouri* belongs in Pearl Harbor together with the USS *Arizona.* I am sure the people of Hawaii will treat the gallant *Missouri* with the utmost respect and dignity she deserves when she pulls into port at Pearl Harbor."

Coming close ashore at Wonsan, Korea, to deliver gunfire on enemy positions, 7 February 1953. Photo from Naval Historical Center.

The *Missouri's* awesome sixteen-inch guns lay down a bombardment off Chongjin, Korea, in 1950. U.S. Navy photo.

The battleship fires a three-gun salvo from her number two turret at a Korean target, February 1951. Note U.S. flag and the ship's hull number used as identification markings on the forward turret. Photo from Naval Historical Center.

At battle ready, crewmen of starboard midships forty-millimeter quad gun mounts watch as the sixteen-inch/fifty-caliber gun turret fires a salvo at enemy forces at Kansong, Korea, February 1951. Photo from Naval Historical Center.

While a signal officer reads the incoming signal, a signalman flashes an "M."

THE JOURNEY TO PEARL

Bremerton said goodbye to the Mighty Mo, the ship the city had hosted for nearly forty years, on May 23, 1998. The tug *Sea Victory* under Captain Kaare Ogaard and with a crew of seven, began the long tow of the Mighty Mo to Pearl Harbor. The *Sea Victory*, owned by Crowley Marine Services, a West Coast firm, towed the battleship at roughly six knots (about seven miles an hour). Before the departure, a Hawaiian from Seattle, Aupuni Iwi'ula, blessed the *Missouri* with a mixture of sea water from Bremerton and salt from Hawaii, and prayed for the sea to welcome the historic battleship in her new home at Pearl Harbor.

First there was an important stop. The battleship was towed to Astoria, Oregon, at the mouth of the Columbia River. There she rested in fresh water to kill the marine organisms on her hull. The ship's reception in Astoria was overwhelming, with an estimated 125,000 visitors jamming the area around the ship during her five-day

Below decks, two petty officers tend to the ship's updated propulsion system.

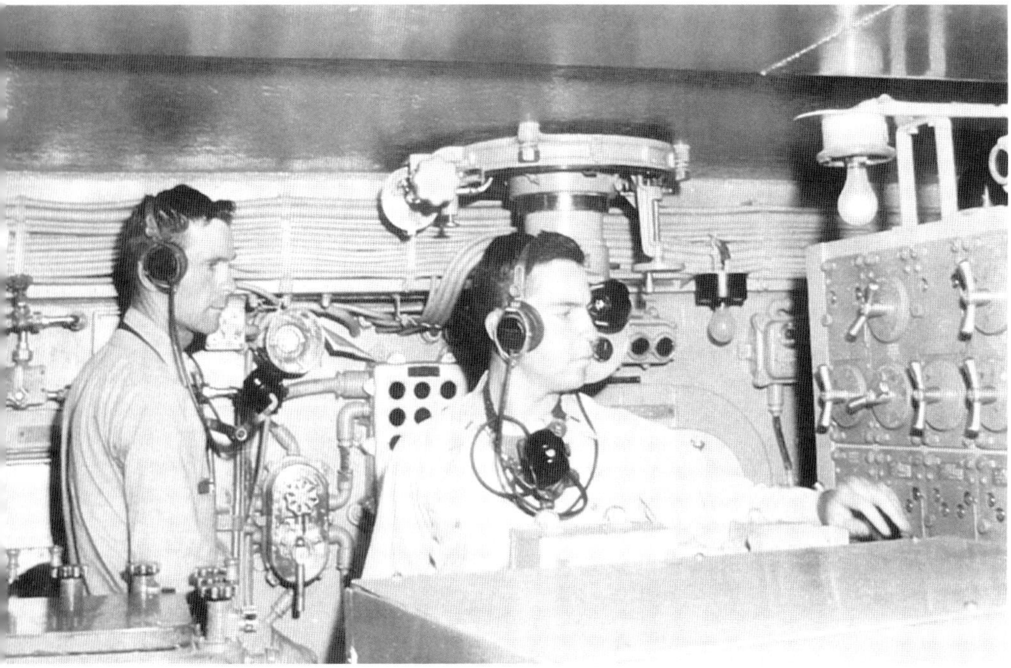

During bombardment operations off Korea, Chief Gunner's Mate W. L. Stull (left) and Ensign R. H. Sprince relay an order to load all guns of turret one, October 1950. Photo from Naval Historical Center.

Excerpts from the surrender document signed at eight minutes after 9:00 a.m. on September 2, 1945, aboard the USS *Missouri* in Tokyo Bay.

"We hereby proclaim the unconditional surrender to the Allied Powers of the Japanese Imperial General Headquarters and of all Japanese armed forces and all armed forces under Japanese control wherever situated . . .

"We hereby command all Japanese forces wherever situated and the Japanese people to cease hostilities forthwith, to preserve and save from damage all ships, aircraft, and military and civil property and to comply with all requirements which may be imposed by the Supreme Commander for the Allied Powers or by agencies of the Japanese Government at his direction . . .

"We hereby command the Japanese Imperial Government and the Japanese Imperial General Headquarters at once to liberate all allied prisoners of war and civilian internees now under Japanese control and to provide for their protection, care, maintenance and immediate transportation to places as directed . . .

"The authority of the Emperor and the Japanese Government to rule the state shall be subject to the Supreme Commander for the Allied Powers who shall take such steps as he deems proper to effectuate these terms of surrender."

stopover. Then it was off again on the twenty-three-hundred-mile journey to Pearl Harbor.

Captain Ogaard and his crew reported no great problems towing the great ship. The seventeen days at sea passed uneventfully. In Hawaii, the USS *Missouri* Memorial Association was busy with final berthing arrangements and answering queries from the public. Roy Yee, then president of the association, was thinking of different ways of showing off the ship to the public. Tom Manuel, association vice president, noted the "frantic" pace of events as the ship drew closer to the Islands.

On June 20, the tug and her 887-foot tow were off Kalaupapa, Molokai, where they paused long enough to dip the U.S. flag and give a whistle salute to the Island in commemoration of the salute rendered in 1908 by President Theodore Roosevelt's "Great White Fleet." Then, on Father's Day, June 21, the tug towed the Mighty Mo past Diamond Head and down the shoreline of Oahu, where thousands jammed the beaches and even stopped traffic in places to get a look at the historic battleship. At 9:00 A.M. the next day, the *Missouri* entered Pearl Harbor and was eased into berth F-5 on Ford Island, the pier built for her in the days when Hawaii hoped to get the ship and her battle group home-ported at Pearl Harbor. Eventually, the ship was to be moved farther down the channel to a permanent mooring at F-3. Meanwhile, a

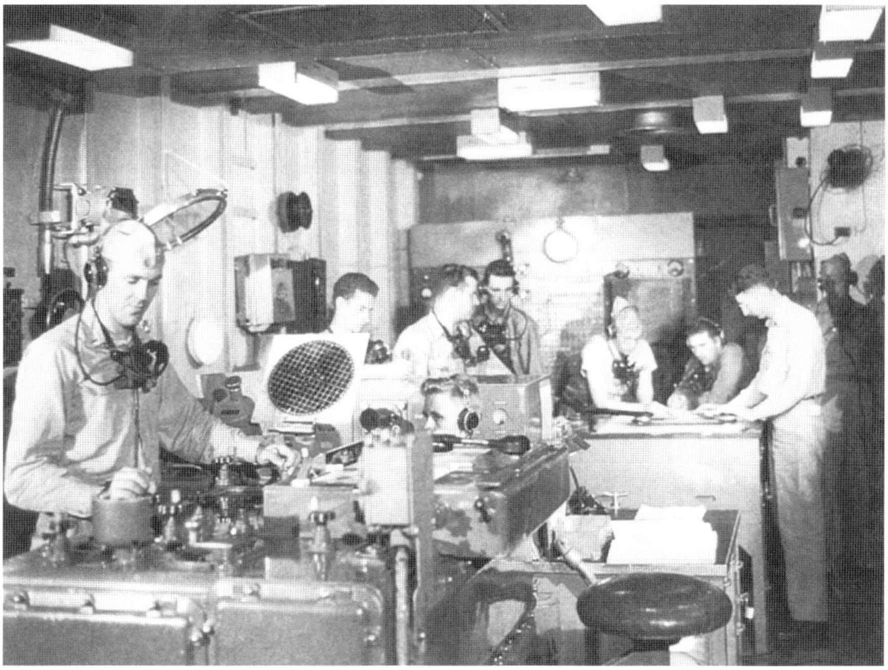

Scene in the ship's main battery plotting room, during operations off Korea, 17 September 1950. Photo from Naval Historical Center.

causeway has been built from the Island of Oahu to Ford Island, to facilitate movement of visitors via trolley to view the great ship.

So the *Missouri* came home, not to end her days but to continue them in a vital new mission—memorial, museum, and reminder that sea power will always be necessary for a nation to preserve its freedoms.

Shortly after reactivation in July 1986, the Mighty Mo glides easily through blue waters. U.S. Navy photo.

Opposite page, top: An overhead view shows the powerful broadside from the ship's fore and aft gun turrets. U.S. Navy photo.

Right: Under heavy attack from kamikazes, this quad-forties gun crew reacts.

At a base in Japan, crewmen load sixteen-inch projectiles aboard *Missouri* to be used for Korean War bombardment, February 1951. Note shell carts used to move the projectiles on the battleship's upper deck. Photo from Naval Historical Center.

During gunnery exercises in 1987, the *Missouri* fires a sixteen-inch projectile from turret one. Photo from Naval Historical Center.

February 9, 1990, a commercial tug guides her to the Naval Air Station at San Diego, California. Photo from Naval Historical Center.

The USS *Missouri* entering Pearl Harbor and approaching her berth at Ford Island. The white, parabolic structure in the foreground is the memorial spanning the sunken battleship USS *Arizona*. U.S. Navy photo.

The Mighty Mo at rest, silhouetted by the falling sun, Pearl Harbor.

The waters of Pearl Harbor are calm and the winds gentle. The great ship lies under a wash of sunlight darkened only momentarily by the passing of puffy cumulus clouds on a typical trade wind day. Not far away the graceful memorial spanning the sunken battleship Arizona *glistens and there is the occasional snap of the American flag in the quickening breeze.*

The Missouri's *signs of age and war are disappearing as the rust and scars give way to cleansing and new paint. It is a cosmetic improvement, for none of the great ship's grandeur has ever been lost, and the visitor senses that as the ship rides easily at her mooring. The big guns which spoke with such devastating effect in so many places are silenced forever, but their sense of menace remains. The decks which knew the tred of so many sailors for so long a time now know those ghostly footsteps, heard faintly by the sensitive visitor.*

She is not dead, or even sleeping. The USS Missouri *(BB-63) is continuing her tradition of service by her role as a memorial and a museum, and by her massive presence that recalls the era of the great ships, and why they were built, and why the sea will always loom large in the defense of America, a sea-going nation. The* Missouri *is active by her very existence, positive in her grace and function.*

The sun moves to another part of the sky and the shadows lengthen along the decks and the last visitor of the day walks away. The sun sets gold and red, and soon a great yellow moon rises to throw its pale light over the last battleship.

Being eased toward her berth, the USS *Missouri* completes her twenty-three-hundred-mile sea trek to Hawaii on 22 June 1998. In the first three months the ship was open to the public, almost ninety thousand visitors came on board to admire the last battleship. U.S. Navy photo.

ACKNOWLEDGMENTS

Various Navy personnel and commands assisted with the preparation of this overview of the USS *Missouri* and the author wishes to thank the Department of the Navy. Special thanks go to Lieutenant Commander R. J. Gibbons, public affairs officer for Navy Region Hawaii. To confirm some data, Paul Stillwell's massive and definitive work, *Battleship Missouri, An Illustrated History*, published by the U.S. Naval Institute of Annapolis, Maryland, was an invaluable tool. That book will remain the classic work on the *Missouri* and is highly recommended.

Some media accounts, especially from the dailies *Honolulu Advertiser* and *Honolulu Star-Bulletin*, were useful, particularly in their coverage of the ship's arrival in Honolulu. The author is pleased that Old Navy Hands participated in this book, among them Harold Estes, Gene Ellis, and Bill Aull. Thanks also to Sally Davis at the Donning Company, for support. Finally, material prepared by the USS *Missouri* Memorial Association was important in establishing a perspective on efforts to bring the battleship to her final port in Hawaii.

The Writer

Commander Scott C. S. Stone (USNR-Ret.) is a national prize-winning novelist, a biographer, historian, and veteran foreign correspondent. Pursuing dual careers, his military service includes combat in two wars, sea duty on a destroyer and a cruiser, and with paramilitary units sailing Chinese junks in wartime. He has had twenty-one books published prior to this one. Commander Stone has maintained a residence in Hawaii for more than forty years while traveling and living in foreign areas.

The Illustrator

Arthur E. (Gene) Ellis is as well known for his versatility as for the quality of his work. He is illustrator, animator, cinematographer, sculptor, still photographer, and has worked as art director on several feature films. He has traveled extensively, including a photo journey to the South Pole. Ellis is a veteran of the Navy's famed Pacific Combat Camera Group.

The Photo Editor

Bill Aull has spent much of his life in creative capacities, primarily as a college-level teacher of creative writing. Also a Navy veteran, Aull is accustomed to wearing several hats, as literary agent, public relations specialist, and technical editor of a literary quarterly. He makes his home in the Pacific Northwest.

The USS *Missouri* Memorial Association is a private Hawaii-based 501 (c) 3 nonprofit organization designated by the Navy as caretaker of the Battleship *Missouri*. It is not supported with government funding. For more information, contact:

USS *Missouri* Memorial Association, Inc.
P.O. Box 6339 Honolulu, HI 96818
Ph. (808) 423-2263
Fax (808) 423-0700
Website: www. ussmissouri.com